my world of science

Scientific Instruments

Published in the United States of America by Cherry Lake Publishing
Ann Arbor, Michigan
www.cherrylakepublishing.com

Reading Adviser: Marla Conn MS, Ed., Literacy specialist, Read-Ability, Inc.
Content Adviser: Brittany Burchard M.Ed., Science teacher
Book Design: Jennifer Wahi
Illustrator: Jeff Bane

Photo Credits: ©Dmitry Morgan/Shutterstock, 5; ©Rawpixel.com/Shutterstock, 7; ©plenoy m/Shutterstock, 9;
©FrameStockFootages/Shutterstock, 11; ©Jesse Davis/Shutterstock, 13; ©wavebreakmedia/Shutterstock, 15;
©Cultura Motion/Shutterstock, 17; ©Rawpixel.com/Shutterstock, 19; ©wavebreakmedia/Shutterstock, 21;
©AlesiaKan/Shutterstock, 23; Cover, 8, 14, 20, Jeff Bane

Library of Congress Cataloging-in-Publication Data

Names: Marsico, Katie, author.
Title: Scientific instruments / by Katie Marsico.
Description: Ann Arbor, Michigan : Cherry Lake Publishing, [2018] | Series:
   My world of science | Audience: K to grade 3.
Identifiers: LCCN 2018003115| ISBN 9781534128910 (hardcover) | ISBN
   9781534132115 (pbk.) | ISBN 9781534130616 (pdf) | ISBN 9781534133815
   (hosted ebook)
Subjects: LCSH: Scientific apparatus and instruments--Juvenile literature.
Classification: LCC Q184 .M37 2018 | DDC 502.8/4--dc23
LC record available at https://lccn.loc.gov/2018003115

Printed in the United States of America
Corporate Graphics

About the author: Katie Marsico is the author of more than 200 reference books for children and young adults. She lives with her husband and six children near Chicago, Illinois.

About the illustrator: Jeff Bane and his two business partners own a studio along the American River in Folsom, California, home of the 1849 Gold Rush. When Jeff's not sketching or illustrating for clients, he's either swimming or kayaking in the river to relax.

Scientists ask questions.

They use **instruments** to find answers.

Some tools help scientists see things better.

One tool is a microscope.

It makes small objects look larger.

People view **cells** with a microscope.

Most cells are tiny and hard to see.

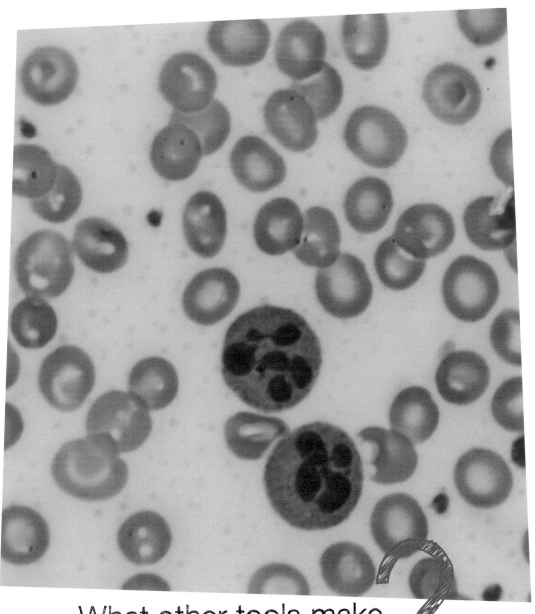

What other tools make objects look larger?

Stars are far away. It's hard to see them.

A telescope makes stars seem closer.

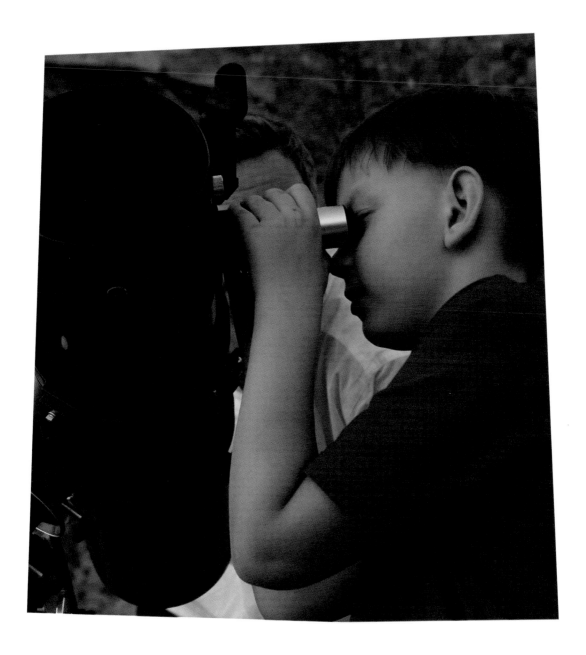

Scientists use instruments to **measure**.

A ruler measures length.

A scale measures weight.

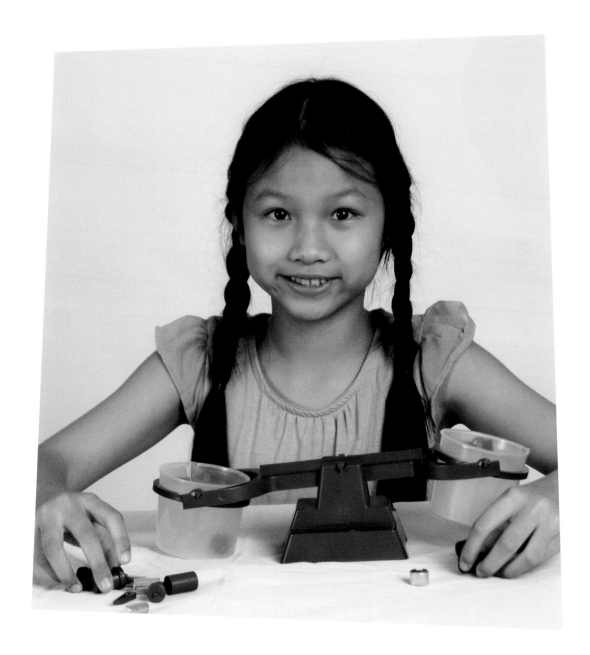

Scientists measure **temperature**, too.

They use a thermometer.

When have you used a thermometer?

Beakers are measuring tools.

So are **eyedroppers**.

Some instruments keep scientists safe.

Goggles cover their eyes.

Gloves guard their hands.

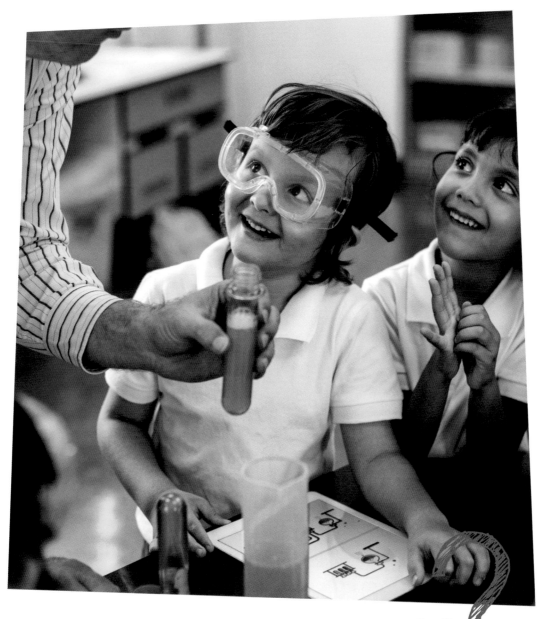

What do you do to stay safe?

Scientists use computers to gather ideas.

Some scientists use scientific instruments. They ask questions. They look for answers.

What would you like to study next?

glossary

beakers (BEE-kuhrz) deep containers that are used for holding and measuring liquids

cells (SELLZ) the smallest units of living matter

eyedroppers (EYE-drahp-urz) tools that measure liquid by drops

instruments (IN-struh-muhnts) tools made to do a certain thing, especially something hard

measure (MEZH-ur) to find out the size or weight of something

scientists (SYE-uhn-tists) people who study nature and the world we live in

temperature (TEM-pur-uh-chur) how hot or cold something is

index

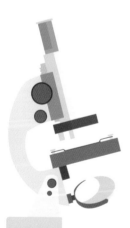